healthy cooking for your kids

healthy
cooking for
your
kids

Sarah Banbery

This is a Parragon Publishing Book
First published in 2006

Parragon Publishing
Queen Street House
4 Queen Street
Bath BA1 1HE, UK

ISBN: 1-40545-020-7
Printed in China

Produced by the Bridgewater Book Company Ltd

Recipe photography: Clive Bozzard-Hill
Home economist: Sandra Baddeley
Illustrator: Anna Andrews

The Bridgewater Book Company would like to thank the following
for permission to reproduce copyright material: Jupiter Images
Corporation, front cover (bottom, second from left and second
from right) and pages 3, 5 (top), 6 (top left, middle left and
middle right), 8 (left and middle), 10 (bottom left, bottom middle
and bottom right), 12 (second from top, and bottom), 16 (top
left and bottom right), 17 and the front cover (second from left,
second from right); Image 100, page 9 (middle); and Laureen
March/Corbis, page 13.

Note
This book uses imperial, metric, or US cup measurements. Follow
the same units of measurement throughout; do not mix imperial
and metric. All spoon measurements are level: teaspoons are
assumed to be 5 ml, and tablespoons are assumed to be 15 ml.
Unless otherwise stated, milk is assumed to be whole, eggs and
individual vegetables such as potatoes are medium, and pepper
is freshly ground black pepper.

Recipes using raw or very lightly cooked eggs should be avoided
by infants, the elderly, pregnant women, convalescents, and
anyone suffering from an illness. Whole nuts and seeds are not
recommended for children under five years of age. Nut butters
and finely chopped or crushed nuts and seeds are fine for babies
of six months or older, unless there has been a history of allergies
to nuts or seeds within the family. If you have any concerns,
please discuss it with your health practitioner.

contents

1 nutrition for kids   6

2 breakfast   18

3 lunches and lunchboxes   38

4 party   64

5 family meals   84

6 treats   106

1

nutrition for kids

introduction

Healthy Cooking for Your Kids is designed to provide a range of delicious and easy recipes that will help you to give your child a balanced and nutritious diet. Good nutrition will not only benefit your child's health, but may also improve his or her behavior and general well-being. Good—or bad—nutrition has an impact on the future health and development of your child and it is vital that healthy eating habits are established early, because they will then, most probably, last a lifetime.

What children eat directly affects their physical and mental development and is also crucial in fighting off illness. Ideally, children should have plenty of energy and a good capacity for mental concentration, as well as healthy teeth, skin, and hair.

Children should be introduced to the widest variety of foods possible as soon as they begin eating solids in order to experience new flavors and textures and to develop an early interest in food. Regular meals and healthy snacks should provide a framework for a good diet with the right balance of nutrients and calorie content.

ESTABLISHING HEALTHY APPROACHES TO FOOD

Food can often become a battleground for parents and kids, so it is important to consider your own attitudes to food—your approach to food and eating, and that of the whole family, can affect the way your child views food. Try to avoid expressing a dislike for any particular food and make an effort to eat together as a family. Also avoid excluding any food from your child's diet, but keep certain foods to a minimum—processed foods invariably have high levels of fat, salt, and sugar, so it is better when possible to cook your child's food from scratch with fresh ingredients. Try not to use food as a bribe or a reward, but keep a balanced approach and avoid making certain foods more attractive by banning them. Once a food is banned, it inevitably becomes much more desirable. Try to include healthy "treats" in your child's everyday diet to counteract the lure of unhealthy snack foods.

Presentation is often the key to interesting your child in new foods. For instance, boiled or steamed vegetables may be very healthy, but many children find them unappetizing, so think around the problem by "hiding" vegetables in pasta sauces or on homemade pizzas. Taking kids along to farmers' markets or farm stores to see the range and variety of fruit and vegetables and where they come from may help interest your child in sampling them. Similarly, getting children involved in cooking is also a great way to encourage them to try new foods. The whole experience of planning, shopping, cooking, and eating can be a fun way to help develop your child's palate, and understanding where food comes from and participating in its choice and preparation will help to promote a healthy interest in food.

ACHIEVING A BALANCED DIET

A healthy diet is one that includes a rich diversity of foods, which will ensure that your child gets an adequate amount of all the major food groups. As a rough guide, your child should be having 2–4 portions of fruit, 3–5 portions of vegetables, 4–6 portions of grains/potatoes, 2–4 portions of calcium-rich foods, 2–4 portions of protein, and 1–2 portions of healthy fats/oils each day. If this forms the basis for the way you feed your children, you will be providing them with the right balance of vitamins and minerals to keep them in good health.

Fruit and Vegetables

Include as many different kinds of fruit and vegetables as possible in your child's diet, because they are a rich source of energy, providing essential B vitamins, iron, minerals, and fiber, as well as phytonutrients. Your child will get natural sugars from fresh and dried fruit, which should replace refined sugars in candies, cakes, and cookies.

Grains and Potatoes

Try to include unrefined and whole grain foods, and avoid "white" or refined foods such as white bread and pasta. Whole wheat bread and rolls, whole wheat flour, whole wheat pasta, porridge oats, potatoes, sweet potatoes, and noodles are all good sources of iron, B vitamins, and fiber, and will provide your child with energy.

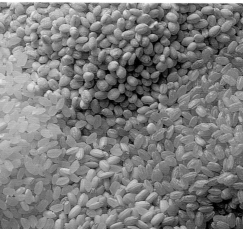

Calcium-Rich Foods

Growing children need calcium for strong bones and teeth and therefore require a range of calcium-rich foods in their diet, such as milk, soymilk, cheese, yogurt, tofu, and canned oily fish such as sardines, as well as green leafy vegetables, nuts, and seeds.

Protein

Protein is important for growth and development, and good sources include lean cuts of meat, chicken, and turkey, fish, eggs, beans, lentils, nuts, and seeds.

Fats/Oils

Avoid giving your child too many animal fats and concentrate on healthy oils that will provide omega-3 and omega-6 fats, which are important for brain development and good eyesight. Good sources are olive, canola, and sunflower oils, nut oils, nuts, seeds, oily fish such as mackerel and salmon, and avocados.

Salt and Sugar

It is important to monitor the amount of salt and sugar that your child is eating, because these can have adverse effects on your child's health. Salt contains sodium, and too much can lead to health problems such as raised blood pressure. Sugary foods contribute to tooth decay and have a high-calorie content. Processed foods often have high levels of salt and sugar, so homemade food is the obvious way to control your child's intake of both.

Buy salt-reduced versions of foods such as tomato ketchup, soy sauce, and stock, and replace potato chips and salted nuts with dried fruit and raw nuts. Make your own pasta sauces and soups so that you can regulate the salt content.

Recommended Levels of Salt

Under 7 years	no more than 3 g per day
7–10 years	no more than 5 g per day
11 years and older	no more than 6 g per day

Sodas, cookies, cakes, candies, chocolate, and desserts are the obvious sources of sugar, but there may be high levels of sugar in processed foods such as ready-made pizzas, ready meals, cereals, canned foods, chicken nuggets, and bottled sauces. Check labels for sugar content and try to accustom your child to the natural sugar in fresh and dried fruit, honey, and maple syrup.

Recommended Levels of Sugar

4–6 years	40 g per day
7–10 years	46 g per day
11–14 years	50 g per day

DEALING WITH INTOLERANCES AND ALLERGIES

Research into the increased incidence of food-related intolerance and allergies in children suggests that many may be controlled or eliminated by the right diet or simply restricting certain foods. Additives in food have been shown to provoke allergic reactions in some children and certain food colors and preservatives cause hyperactivity in others. If you suspect that your child may have a serious allergy, speak to your doctor. If there is a history of allergies in your family, avoid giving any nuts or nut products to children under the age of three and, in any case, whole nuts should not be given to the under-fives. Speak to your doctor about any concerns regarding allergies or intolerance symptoms, and take expert advice on compiling a diet that may restrict certain foods as necessary.

PRACTICAL STRATEGIES FOR HEALTHY EATING

Evidence suggests that a diet reliant on processed foods and with little fruit or vegetables can seriously affect a child's physical development as well as behavior and concentration levels. While it may sometimes seem an effort to provide fresh, wholesome food, it really does make a difference to your child's health now and in the future. So having established that fresh food is best, how can you make sure that your child eats the foods that you choose? It is invaluable to have some strategies on hand for coping with problems associated with feeding your child the balanced diet he or she needs.

While the focus of this book is on healthy eating, it is important not to become obsessive and stressed over what your child is eating—you can't expect your child to like all foods, and as long as she or he is willing to try everything and then perhaps rejects the odd food, that should encourage a relaxed attitude to eating. As soon as your child reaches the age of one year, your goal should be to increase the variety of foods offered. For young children, bear in mind that the choice to eat or not may well just be a way of asserting their budding independence and becomes one of the few things in their lives over which they have any control.

Don't overload their plates—it is off-putting for children to be presented with huge piles of food with you expecting them to eat it all. Instead, take a little time to present their food well and give them manageable portions—better that they ask for a little more than reject the whole plate. Don't press children to eat what they obviously dislike, but also don't give in to pressure to give them just what they want. Try not to make too much of an issue about it—if they refuse to eat what they are offered, simply remove it without a fuss, and don't offer a replacement. However, continue to encourage them to try new flavors. Avoid commenting on what your children eat or discussing weight or calories in front of them. And do persevere—sometimes it may take three or four attempts before a child will develop a taste for a certain food and it can be the seemingly unlikely foods, such as olives, that become favorites. Try to avoid classifying foods as "children's", since this excludes certain foods. "Adult" foods may appeal to many children, because they often like strong flavors.

Reaching the Five-A-Day Target

Getting your child to eat the required five portions of fruit and vegetables a day may seem like a challenge, but once you realize that a portion is not too big, it will seem less daunting. A child's portion of fruit or vegetables is roughly the amount the child can hold in one hand—just increase the amount as the child grows. Then if you consider that you can actually often incorporate a significant amount of fruit or vegetables in one recipe, the five-a-day goal becomes far more realistic. For instance, the Creamy Tomato Soup on page 40 contains five different fresh vegetables, but since it is creamy and smooth, even the most veg-phobic child would struggle to identify them. Recipes like this, which incorporate vegetables rather than serving them as a side dish, tend to be more acceptable to children generally. So, if your child starts the day with a glass of fresh fruit juice, has chopped fruit for two snacks, and two or three more portions included in his or her meals, you're reached the target!

Be creative and add vegetables to kids' favorites such as mashed potatoes—you can easily add other root vegetables or puréed greens without much extra effort. You can also incorporate plenty of vegetables in Roast Vegetable Lasagna (see page 94) and Burritos

(see page 88) and all manner of other pies, as well as sandwich fillers, toppings, and sauces. Children often prefer their vegetables raw, so colorful strips of raw vegetables are idea for lunchboxes, and fun "Party Straws" of vegetables and fruit go down well (see page 83). Include fruit in as many desserts as possible–if your child loves ice cream, offer a small portion of organic ice cream with a homemade fruit purée, or make colorful and delicious Tropical Fruit Tarts or Mini Fruit Trifles (see pages 127 and 119). You can also make very healthy, pure fruit lollipops by freezing fresh puréed fruit such as mango, strawberry, and raspberry (see Yogurt Lollipops on page 114).

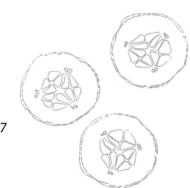

Make sure you vary the fruit and vegetables, mixing up the colors. In fact, get your children to choose which fruit and vegetables they will have when shopping, but don't worry if they refuse some items, as long as they have a good mix. Letting your children help you choose what to buy and also helping themselves at the table makes them feel that they have some control.

HEALTHY EATING FOR LIFE
It is virtually impossible to regulate everything that your children eat, especially as they get older, but by encouraging good habits early on, you stand a much better chance of your children carrying them through to adulthood. By making even small changes to your children's diets, you can make a big difference, and putting in the effort at this early stage really does have its rewards and can influence the quality of your children's whole lives.

We all know that breakfast is an important meal, but it is doubly so for children. Breakfast is a vital meal for good nutrition and sets your child up for the day ahead. It should ideally include both complex carbohydrates and protein, and should really kick-start your child's metabolism.

2 breakfast

Many commercially produced breakfast cereals tend to have high levels of sugar and salt and should be avoided. If you do choose bought cereal, try to make sure that it has whole grains and no added sugar or salt, and add some chopped fresh or dried fruit. A homemade breakfast can be better for your child and doesn't have to be time consuming to prepare when you have a busy morning. Many of the recipes in this chapter can be put together quickly or made ahead, and will provide your child with a healthy, balanced start to the day.

Complex carbohydrates that release sugars into the bloodstream slowly will keep your child going throughout the morning and oats are a great source. They are featured here in homemade granola and porridge, which are easy to make and offer the opportunity to incorporate fruit and nuts to provide a good balance of nutrients for your child. A fruit muffin with added bran and a fruit smoothie also makes a great start to the day and your child can easily get involved in making these.

If your child asks for toast, whole wheat bread is the healthy option. Try out a variety of nut butters, which are available from health food stores and some supermarkets—cashew nut or almond make good alternatives to peanut and work well with banana, or chopped apple or apricot. Choose fruit compotes with natural sugars rather than commercially made jellies or preserves, which tend to have lots of added refined sugar. To make your own compote, just add a little honey or maple syrup to stewed fresh fruit such as apple and pear, or dark berries and strawberries.

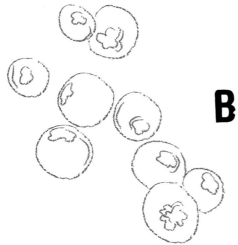

Blueberry Bran Muffins

Preheat the oven to 350°F/180°C. Line 10 holes of a muffin pan with muffin paper cases.

Mix the flours, bran, baking powder, baking soda, and salt together in a bowl and stir in the sugar. Whisk the honey, egg, and buttermilk together in a pitcher.

Pour the wet ingredients into the dry and stir briefly to combine. Don't overmix—the batter should still be a little lumpy. Fold in the blueberries.

Spoon the batter into the paper cases and bake in the preheated oven for 20 minutes until risen and lightly browned.

Remove the muffins from the oven and let cool in the pan. Serve warm or cold.

generous 1 cup white
   all-purpose flour
scant ¾ cup light brown
   self-rising flour
1 tbsp oat bran
2 tsp baking powder
½ tsp baking soda
pinch of salt
¼ cup packed raw brown sugar
1 tbsp honey
1 large egg
scant 1 cup buttermilk
1⅛ cups fresh blueberries

Almond and Golden Raisin Crêpes with Raspberries

2 tbsp unsalted butter

1 large egg

1¼ cups buttermilk

½ tsp vanilla extract

generous ½ cup white
    all-purpose flour

generous ⅜ cup whole wheat
    all-purpose flour

1 tsp baking soda

¼ cup ground almonds

scant ½ cup golden raisins

2 tsp vegetable oil

1¼ cups fresh raspberries

⅜ cup toasted slivered almonds

Melt the butter in a small pan over low heat.

Whisk the egg, buttermilk, and vanilla extract together in a bowl, add the melted butter, and stir to combine.

In a separate bowl, mix the flours, baking soda, and ground almonds together and then stir in the egg mixture and golden raisins.

Heat half the oil in a large, nonstick skillet and drop in 3–4 separate tablespoons of the batter—each will make a 4-inch/10-cm crêpe, so don't overcrowd the skillet. Cook for 2 minutes on each side, then remove from the skillet and keep warm in a low oven while you cook the remaining crêpes. Use the remaining oil to do this.

Serve warm with the raspberries, sprinkled with the toasted almonds.

Serves 1

Sunshine Toast

Using a cookie cutter, cut a hole in the center of the slice of bread, large enough to hold the egg.

Heat the oil in a nonstick skillet and cook the mushrooms and tomato, cut-sides down, for 3–4 minutes until the mushrooms are beginning to brown. Turn the tomato over.

Make a space in the middle of the skillet and add the bread. Crack the egg open and carefully pour it into the hole in the bread. Reduce the heat and cook slowly until cooked through.

Season everything to taste with pepper and serve the sunshine toast with the mushrooms and tomato alongside.

1 slice whole wheat bread
1 tbsp olive oil
2–3 mushrooms, sliced
1 tomato, halved
1 small egg
pepper

Serves 1

Fruit Smoothies

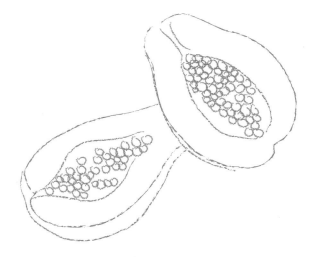

Place all the ingredients in a blender or food processor and process until combined and frothy. Pour into a tall glass and serve immediately.

Mango and Papaya
As for Berry, but substitute ½ pitted, peeled, and chopped mango and ½ seeded, peeled, and chopped papaya for the berries and black currants.

Banana, Peach, and Strawberry
As for Berry, but substitute ½ peeled and sliced banana, ½ pitted, peeled, and chopped peach, and 3 hulled strawberries for the berries and black currants.

Berry
1¼ cups whole milk
  or soymilk
2 tbsp plain yogurt
1 tbsp maple syrup
3 blackberries
⅜ cup blueberries
¼ cup black currants

Cereal Fruit Cupcakes

7 tbsp unsalted butter

⅜ cup honey

1¾ cups oatmeal

1¾ cups unsweetened crispy rice

1 tbsp sesame seeds

3½ oz/100 g mixed dried fruit,
    such as pears, mangoes, apples,
    and cranberries, chopped

⅓ cup shelled pecans, chopped

Melt the butter and honey in a small pan over low heat.

Mix the oatmeal, crispy rice, sesame seeds, dried fruit, and chopped nuts together in a bowl, add the melted butter and honey, and stir to combine.

Spoon into 12 cake paper cases and press down well. Let chill for 6 hours before serving.

Crunchy Yogurt

This recipe will make more granola than you need. Make the granola in advance and keep it in an airtight container.

Preheat the oven to 350°F/180°C.

Mix the oats and honey together in a bowl and spread out on a baking sheet. Bake in the preheated oven for 10–15 minutes, stirring a couple of times, until the oats are lightly browned, then remove from the oven and let cool.

Place the seeds in a mortar and briefly grind with a pestle to break them into smaller pieces. Mix with the cooled oats and the walnuts.

To assemble, put half the pear and mango in a glass and top with half the yogurt and a spoonful of granola. Repeat with the remaining fruit and yogurt and top with more granola.

2⅓ cups rolled oats
2 tbsp honey
2 tbsp pumpkin seeds
2 tbsp sunflower seeds
2 tbsp chopped walnuts
1 small ripe pear, peeled, cored, and chopped
½ ripe mango, pitted, peeled, and chopped
generous ½ cup plain yogurt

Serves 4

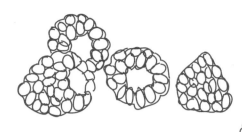

Bircher Granola

The night before serving, mix the oats, wheat germ, and milk together in a bowl, cover with plastic wrap, and let chill overnight.

To serve, stir the oat mixture, add the honey, yogurt, and apple, and mix well.

Spoon into serving bowls, top with the nuts and berries, and drizzle over a little more honey, or fruit purée, if using.

3 cups rolled oats
1 tbsp wheat germ
scant 1 cup whole milk or
    soymilk
2 tbsp honey, plus extra
    for serving (optional)
2 tbsp plain yogurt
1 apple, peeled, cored, and grated
1 cup chopped nuts, such as
    macadamia nuts, cashews,
    or hazelnuts
mixed berries, such as blueberries,
    raspberries, and strawberries
fruit purée, to serve (optional)

Apple and Hazelnut Bread

Grease and line a 1-lb/450-g loaf pan. Put a generous ⅓ cup of the warm water in a pitcher, stir in the sugar and yeast, and leave for 15 minutes.

Mix the flours, salt, nuts, and dried and fresh apple together in a large bowl. Make a well in the center, pour in the yeast mixture, and gradually work into the flour mixture. Mix in the remaining warm water and bring together to form a soft dough.

Turn out onto a floured counter and knead briefly. Shape the dough into a rectangle and place in the prepared pan. Cover with a warm, damp cloth and set aside in a warm place for 40 minutes until the dough has risen.

Meanwhile, preheat the oven to 400°F/200°C. Remove the cloth and bake the loaf in the preheated oven for 40 minutes. Carefully lift out of the pan and return the loaf to the oven, upside down, for 10–15 minutes—the loaf should sound hollow when tapped on the bottom.

Remove from the oven and let cool on a wire rack. Slice and serve spread with honey, and sliced banana or nut butter. Store wrapped in foil for up to three days, or freeze for up to a month.

butter, for greasing

1½ cups warm water

1 tsp golden superfine sugar

1 x ¼-oz/7-g sachet active dry yeast

generous 2¾ cups white all-purpose flour, plus extra for dusting

generous 2¾ cups light brown self-rising flour

½ tsp sea salt

generous ¾ cup toasted hazelnuts, chopped

1¾ oz/50 g dried apple, chopped

1 eating apple, grated

To serve
honey
sliced banana or nut butter

Mini Cheese and Herb Muffins

2⅛ cups baby spinach leaves

5½ heaping tbsp butter

1¼ oz/35 g Parmesan cheese,
    finely grated

1 tbsp chopped fresh herbs, such
    as chives, parsley, or tarragon

scant ¾ cup white all-purpose flour

scant ¾ cup light brown
    self-rising flour

½ tsp baking soda

pinch of salt

2 tsp baking powder

1 large egg

scant 1 cup buttermilk

Preheat the oven to 400°F/200°C. Line two 12-hole mini muffin pans with mini muffin paper cases.

Put the spinach in a colander and pour boiling water from a kettle over the leaves to wilt them. Let cool, then squeeze all the liquid out until the spinach is very dry. Mince.

Melt the butter in a small pan over low heat, then let cool. Mix the cheese, herbs, flours, baking soda, salt, and baking powder together in a bowl, then stir in the spinach.

Whisk the melted butter with the egg and buttermilk in a pitcher, pour into the dry ingredients, and stir briefly to combine. Don't overmix—the batter should still be a little lumpy.

Spoon a teaspoon of the batter into each of the paper cases and bake in the preheated oven for 12 minutes.

Remove from the oven and let cool in the pan. Serve warm or cold.

Buttered Cinnamon Apples on Fruit Toast

1 tbsp unsalted butter

½ tsp ground cinnamon

1 apple, cored and sliced

1 slice fruit bread

maple syrup, to serve

Melt the butter in a pan over low heat and stir in the cinnamon. Add the apple and stir well to coat.

Preheat the broiler and line the broiler pan with foil. Spread the buttered apple over the broiler pan. Cook under the broiler until the apple is just beginning to brown. Toast the fruit bread and serve with the apple piled on top, drizzled with a little maple syrup.

Serves 1

Baked Eggs with Ham and Tomato

Preheat the oven to 350°F/180°C. Heat the oil in a pan and cook the leek for 5–6 minutes until soft.

Place the leek in the bottom of a ramekin and top with the ham. Crack and pour in the egg, then top with the cheese and tomato.

Bake in the preheated oven for 10 minutes until the egg is set. Remove the ramekin from the oven, let cool a little, wrap in a cloth, and serve.

1 tsp olive oil
½ small leek, chopped
2 slices wafer-thin ham, chopped
1 egg
1 oz/25 g Cheddar cheese, grated
2 slices tomato

Serves 1

Fruity Maple Porridge

Mix the milk and oatmeal together in a pan and cook over medium heat, stirring, for 8–10 minutes.

Serve drizzled with the maple syrup and topped with the fresh fruit, with a little more milk if needed.

To make a breakfast brûlée, preheat the broiler and put the chopped fruit in the bottom of a ramekin. Top with the cooked porridge and a spoonful of brown sugar and place under the broiler until the sugar has melted and caramelized. Let chill before serving.

¾ cup whole milk or soymilk, plus extra for serving (optional)
½ cup oatmeal
1 tbsp maple syrup or honey
mixed fresh fruit, such as apples, pears, bananas, peaches, mangoes, strawberries, and raspberries, prepared and chopped

Coming up with a varied, interesting, and tempting lunch or lunchbox for your child is a daily challenge. A healthy and delicious lunchbox that is filling, nutritious yet also enjoyable is important, because it should provide your child with the energy to sustain her or him right through the afternoon.

3 lunches and lunchboxes

Kids' lunchboxes should contain healthy foods that will nourish them and keep them energized. Lunch should provide a third of your child's daily intake of protein, carbohydrate, fiber, vitamins, and minerals, so it needs to be really appetizing and variety is the watchword. A healthy lunchbox should include a portion of fresh fruit and vegetables, plus one portion each of protein, carbohydrate, and a calcium-rich food such as cheese, yogurt, or milk. If you pack some fruit, and a no-added-sugar fruit drink or water, plus a healthy sandwich or salad, your child will have a tasty, balanced meal. Homemade noodle, pasta, and couscous salads in pots are great served cold in a lunchbox with plenty of added vegetables, and homemade biscuits and cookies are a sweet treat. However, as this chapter shows, all sorts of other foods work well in lunchboxes. There are also many good foods prepackaged to fit into lunchboxes, such as mini containers of fresh and dried fruit, mini cheese portions, and small pots of yogurt or cream cheese. Nuts and vegetable chips make healthy substitutes for potato chips. Besides fruit juice or water to drink, a fruit smoothie or a milk shake is a good option—avoid sodas or fruit squashes with sugar.

Getting children involved in planning and preparing lunch can make a difference to the way they feel about eating it. Baking cookies or tartlets at the weekend or planning the toppings for homemade muffin pizzas can be fun and gets children involved in thinking about food and cooking.

Creamy Tomato Soup

1 tbsp butter

½ red onion, minced

1 leek, chopped

1 garlic clove, crushed

1 carrot, peeled and grated

1 potato, peeled and grated

1¼ cups low-salt vegetable stock

1 lb 2 oz/500 g ripe tomatoes,
   peeled, seeded, and chopped

1 tbsp tomato paste

⅔ cup whole milk

sea salt and pepper

snipped chives, to garnish
   (optional)

whole wheat rolls, to serve

Melt the butter in a large pan over low heat and cook the onion, leek, and garlic for 10 minutes, or until very soft but not browned.

Add the carrot and potato and cook for 5 minutes. Add the stock and bring up to simmering point.

Add the tomatoes and tomato paste and season to taste with salt and pepper. Let simmer for 15 minutes until the vegetables are very soft. Add the milk and warm through, then transfer the soup to a blender or food processor and process until very smooth. You can pass the soup through a strainer at this stage, if you like.

Return the soup to the rinsed-out pan and reheat gently. Garnish the soup with snipped chives, if desired, and serve with whole wheat rolls.

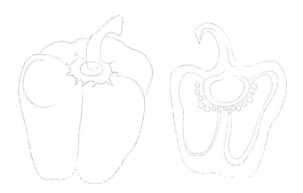

Serves 2

Sesame Noodle Stir-Fry

Mix the vinegar, soy sauce, tomato ketchup, orange juice, and honey together in a pitcher, add the cornstarch, and stir until well combined.

Heat the oil in a nonstick skillet and stir-fry the chicken strips for 3–4 minutes. Add the vegetables and stir-fry for 4–5 minutes.

Add the cornstarch mixture and bring to a boil, stirring constantly, then reduce the heat and let simmer for 1 minute until thickened.

Meanwhile, prepare the noodles according to the package directions, drain, and add to the skillet along with the sesame seeds. Mix well. Serve hot or cold.

1 tsp red wine vinegar

1 tbsp low-salt soy sauce

1 tbsp low-sugar and -salt
   tomato ketchup

2 tbsp orange juice

1 tsp honey

1 tsp cornstarch

1 tbsp vegetable oil

3½ oz/100 g skinless, boneless
   chicken breast, cut into strips

2 scallions, finely sliced

2 oz/55 g baby corn,
   halved lengthwise

1 carrot, cut into thin sticks

½ red bell pepper, seeded and
   chopped

½ zucchini, chopped

1¾ oz/50 g bean thread noodles

2 tsp sesame seeds

Pita Pockets with Hummus and Salad

14 oz/400 g canned chickpeas,
    drained and liquid set aside

1 garlic clove, chopped

3 tbsp olive oil

2 tbsp sesame seed paste

juice of ½ lemon

pinch of paprika

2–4 pita breads

1 tsp vinegar

½ tsp Dijon mustard

¼ iceberg lettuce, finely shredded

1 scallion, chopped

½ yellow bell pepper, seeded
    and chopped

1 large tomato, seeded
    and chopped

2-inch/5-cm piece cucumber,
    chopped

1 carrot, peeled and grated

pepper

To make the hummus, put the chickpeas, garlic, 2 tablespoons of the oil, the sesame seed paste, lemon juice, and a little of the chickpea liquid in a blender or food processor and blend until smooth and creamy. Season to taste with pepper and the paprika.

If serving at home, heat the pita breads according to the package directions and split each one to create a pocket.

To make the dressing, whisk the remaining oil with the vinegar and mustard, and pepper to taste, in a pitcher.

Mix all the salad ingredients together in a bowl, add the dressing, and toss well to coat. Smear the inside of the pita pockets with the hummus, fill with the salad, and serve. For a lunchbox, smear the inside of the unheated pita pockets with hummus, fill with the undressed salad, and wrap well in foil.

Serves 4

Souffléd Baked Potatoes

Preheat the oven to 400°F/200°C. Rub the oil all over the potatoes, place on a baking sheet, and bake in the preheated oven for 1 hour, or until the flesh is soft.

Remove the potatoes from the oven, cut in half lengthwise, and carefully scoop out the flesh into a bowl, keeping the skins intact. Set the skins aside.

Add the milk, butter, Cheddar cheese, and egg yolk to the potato and mash well. Season to taste with salt and pepper. Mix in the ham.

In a separate, grease-free bowl, whisk the egg white until stiff, then fold into the potato mixture.

Pile the potato mixture back into the skins and sprinkle over the Parmesan cheese. Return to the oven and bake for 20 minutes. Serve with salad.

1 tbsp olive oil
2 baking potatoes, scrubbed
2 tbsp whole milk
2 tbsp butter
1 oz/25 g Cheddar or Gruyère
    cheese, grated
1 large egg, separated
2 slices ham, cooked turkey,
    or unsmoked bacon, chopped
2 tbsp finely grated Parmesan
    cheese
sea salt and pepper
salad, to serve

Tortillas with Tuna, Egg, and Corn

1 tbsp plain yogurt

1 tsp olive oil

½ tsp white wine vinegar

½ tsp Dijon mustard

1 large egg, hard-cooked
   and cooled

7 oz/200 g canned tuna in spring
   water, drained

7 oz/200 g canned no-added-sugar
   corn kernels, drained

2 whole wheat flour tortillas

1 container mustard and cress

pepper

To make the dressing, whisk the yogurt, oil, vinegar, and mustard, and pepper to taste, in a pitcher until emulsified and smooth.

Shell the egg, separate the yolk and the white, then mash the yolk and mince the white. Mash the tuna with the egg and dressing, then mix in the corn.

Spread the filling equally over the 2 tortillas and sprinkle over the mustard and cress. Fold in one end and roll up. Wrap in foil for a packed lunch.

Chicken and Apple Bites

1 apple, peeled, cored, and grated

2 skinless, boneless chicken breasts, cut into chunks

½ red onion, minced

1 tbsp minced fresh parsley

scant 1 cup fresh whole wheat bread crumbs

1 tbsp concentrated chicken stock

whole wheat flour, for coating

peanut oil, for pan-frying

Spread the apple out on a clean dish towel and press out all the excess moisture.

Put the chicken, apple, onion, parsley, bread crumbs, and stock in a food processor and pulse briefly until well combined.

Spread the flour out on a plate. Divide the mixture into 20 mini portions, shape each portion into a ball and roll in the flour.

Heat a little oil in a nonstick skillet over medium heat and cook the balls for 5–8 minutes, or until golden brown all over and cooked through. Remove and drain on paper towels. Serve hot, or cold for a lunchbox.

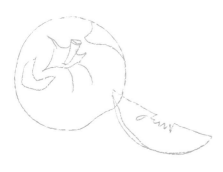

Makes 6

English Muffin Pizzas

Toast the muffins until golden, then let cool.

Mix the tomato paste and pesto together in a small bowl and spread equally over the muffin halves.

Heat the oil in a nonstick skillet and then cook the onion, mushrooms, and zucchini until soft and beginning to brown.

Preheat the broiler to high. Divide the vegetables between the muffins, top with the ham, then the cheese.

Cook under the broiler for 3–4 minutes until the cheese is melted and browned. Serve hot or cold.

3 whole wheat bread English
   muffins, halved
2 tbsp tomato paste
2 tbsp pesto
1 tbsp olive oil
½ red onion, thinly sliced
3 mushrooms, sliced
½ zucchini, thinly sliced
2–3 slices ham or 6 slices salami
scant 1 cup grated Cheddar cheese
   or 6 slices mozzarella cheese

Serves 6

Spanish Omelet

Cook the potatoes in a pan of boiling water for 8–12 minutes until tender. Drain and let cool, then slice.

Heat the oil in a 7–8-inch/18–20-cm skillet with a heatproof handle and cook the sliced onion and red bell pepper until soft. Add the tomatoes and cook for an additional minute.

Add the potatoes to the skillet and spread out evenly. Beat the eggs, milk, and cheese, and salt and pepper to taste, in a bowl and pour over the potato mixture. Cook for 4–5 minutes until the eggs are set underneath.

Meanwhile, preheat the broiler to high. Place the skillet under the broiler and cook the omelet for an additional 3–4 minutes until the eggs are set.

Let cool, then cut into wedges and wrap in foil for a lunchbox.

7 oz/200 g new potatoes

1 tbsp olive oil

1 onion, thinly sliced

1 red bell pepper, seeded and thinly sliced

2 tomatoes, peeled, seeded, and chopped

6 large eggs

1 tbsp milk

1¼ oz/35 g Parmesan cheese, finely grated

sea salt and pepper

Apple and Carrot Muffins

Preheat the oven to 350°F/180°C. Line 12 holes of a muffin pan with muffin paper cases.

Mix the flours, baking powder, baking soda, salt, and nutmeg together in a bowl.

In a separate bowl, mix the apple and carrot together. Stir in the honey and egg, then the buttermilk and sugar. Pour this mixture into the dry ingredients and stir briefly to combine. Don't overmix—the batter should still be a little lumpy.

Spoon the batter into the paper cases and bake in the preheated oven for 20 minutes.

Remove from the oven and let cool in the pan. Serve warm or cold.

generous 1 cup white
  all-purpose flour
scant ¾ cup light brown
  self-rising flour
2 tsp baking powder
½ tsp baking soda
pinch of sea salt
½ tsp ground nutmeg
1 apple, peeled, cored, and grated
½ carrot, peeled and grated
4 tbsp honey
1 large egg, beaten
scant 1 cup buttermilk
4 tbsp raw brown sugar

Sandwiches and Wraps

Use as many varieties of breads as possible to add interest. Choose whole wheat bread or rolls, whole wheat pita breads, tortillas, rye bread, fruit or nut breads, and whole grain bagels and crispbreads, but do not use white processed bread. Some younger children like sandwiches cut into novelty shapes, but you can also make double-decker sandwiches with three different types of whole grain breads, or use mini pita breads, breadsticks (grissini), or tortilla wraps. At home, use Boston lettuce boats to hold the fillings and add as much chopped salad as possible. Also include containers of cherry tomatoes, thin sticks of celery, bell peppers, or carrot, or use straws to make mini vegetable or fruit kabobs. Above all, keep it varied, interesting, and easy to pack and eat.

Try some of the following fillings for sandwiches, mixing and matching to add variety.

cream cheese or goat cheese with snipped chives or chopped scallion

mashed canned salmon, tuna, sardines, or crab with or without mayonnaise

mashed banana

dried fruit, such as apricot, mango, or pear, chopped

canned no-added-sugar corn kernels

chopped hard-cooked egg

avocado

nut butters

honey

hummus

shredded cooked chicken or turkey

lean ham

cooked shrimp

grated carrot and cheese

vegetable pâté

bean pâté

cottage cheese

ricotta cheese

guacamole

Pasta Salad

3½ oz/100 g small whole wheat
   pasta
2 tbsp olive oil
1 tbsp mayonnaise
1 tbsp plain yogurt
2 tbsp pesto
7 oz/200 g canned tuna in spring
   water, drained and flaked
7 oz/200 g canned no-added-sugar
   corn kernels, drained
2 tomatoes, peeled, seeded,
   and chopped
½ green bell pepper, seeded
   and chopped
½ avocado, pitted, peeled,
   and chopped
sea salt and pepper

Cook the pasta in a large pan of boiling water for
8–10 minutes until only just tender. Drain, return to the
pan, and add half the oil. Toss well to coat, then cover
and let cool.

Whisk the mayonnaise, yogurt, and pesto together in a
pitcher, adding a little oil if needed to achieve the desired
consistency. Add a pinch of salt and season to taste
with pepper.

Mix the cooled pasta with the tuna, corn, tomatoes,
green bell pepper, and avocado, add the dressing, and
toss well to coat.

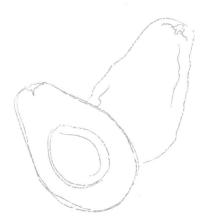

Makes 12

9 tbsp butter, diced and chilled,
plus extra for greasing
generous 1 cup white all-purpose
flour, plus extra for dusting
scant 1 cup whole wheat all-
purpose flour
1 tbsp grated Parmesan cheese
about 1 tbsp cold water
24 cherry tomatoes
1 tbsp olive oil
scant 1 cup whole milk
1¾ oz/50 g Cheddar cheese, grated
generous ⅜ cup ricotta cheese
sea salt and pepper

Cherry Tomato and Cheese Tartlets

Lightly grease a 12-hole muffin pan with butter. Put scant 1 cup of the white flour in a food processor with all the whole wheat flour, a pinch of salt, and 7 tablespoons of the butter, and pulse until the mixture resembles bread crumbs. Tip into a large bowl and stir in the Parmesan cheese. Alternatively, mix the flours with the salt in a large bowl, add the butter, and rub in with your fingertips until the mixture resembles bread crumbs. Then stir in the Parmesan cheese. Add 1 tablespoon cold water, stir, and bring the mixture together to form a dough, adding a little more cold water if needed. Turn out onto a floured counter and knead briefly.

Divide the dough into 12 pieces, roll out each piece into a 4½-inch/12-cm circle and use to line the muffin holes. Let chill for 30 minutes. Meanwhile, preheat the oven to 400°F/200°C. Remove the muffin pan from the refrigerator and line each pastry shell with parchment paper and dried beans. Bake blind in the preheated oven for 10 minutes, then remove from the oven. Lift out the paper and beans and set the pastry shells aside.

Put the tomatoes in a roasting pan and drizzle over the oil. Roast in the oven for 5 minutes. Meanwhile, melt the remaining 2 tablespoons of butter in a pan over low heat. Stir in the remaining white flour and cook, stirring constantly, for 2–3 minutes. Gradually stir in the milk and cook, stirring constantly, until the sauce is thick and smooth. Season to taste with salt and pepper and stir in the Cheddar and ricotta cheeses.

Put 2 tomatoes in each pastry shell and then divide the cheese sauce between the tartlets. Bake in the oven for 15 minutes until golden.

Apricot and Sunflower Seed Cookies

7 tbsp unsalted butter, softened

¼ cup packed raw brown sugar

1 tbsp maple syrup

1 tbsp honey, plus extra for
   brushing

1 large egg, beaten

scant ¾ cup white all-purpose flour,
   plus extra for dusting

1⅜ cups whole wheat
   all-purpose flour

1 tbsp oat bran

½ cup ground almonds

1 tsp ground cinnamon

½ cup no-soak dried
   apricots, chopped

⅛ cup sunflower seeds

Beat the softened butter with the sugar in a large bowl until light and fluffy. Beat in the maple syrup and honey, then the egg.

Add the flours and oat bran, then the almonds and mix well. Add the cinnamon, apricots, and seeds and, with floured hands, mix to a firm dough. Wrap in plastic wrap and let chill for 30 minutes.

Preheat the oven to 350°F/180°C. Roll out the dough on a lightly floured counter to ½ inch/1 cm thick. Using a 2½-inch/6-cm cookie cutter, cut out 20 circles, rerolling the trimmings where possible, and place on a baking sheet. Brush with a little extra honey and bake in the preheated oven for 15 minutes until golden. Remove from the oven and let cool on a wire rack.

Makes 12

Orange and Banana Biscuits

Preheat the oven to 400°F/200°C. Lightly oil a large baking sheet.

Mix the flours, baking powder, and cinnamon together in a large bowl, add the butter, and rub in with your fingertips until the mixture resembles bread crumbs. Stir in the sugar. Make a well in the middle and pour in the milk, add the banana and orange rind, and mix to a soft dough. The dough will be quite wet.

Turn out the dough onto a lightly floured counter and, adding a little more flour if needed, roll out to ¾ inch/ 2 cm thick. Using a 2½-inch/6-cm cookie cutter, cut out 12 biscuits, rerolling the trimmings where possible, and place them on the prepared baking sheet. Brush with milk and bake in the preheated oven for 10–12 minutes.

Remove from the oven and let cool slightly, then halve the biscuits and fill with the raspberries.

sunflower oil, for oiling

generous 1 cup white self-rising
flour, plus extra for dusting, and
rolling if needed

generous 1 cup light brown self-
rising flour

1 tsp baking powder

½ tsp ground cinnamon

5½ heaping tbsp unsalted butter,
diced and chilled

¼ cup packed raw brown sugar

⅔ cup whole milk, plus extra
for brushing

1 ripe banana, peeled and mashed

finely grated rind of 1 orange

1¼ cups fresh raspberries,
lightly mashed

Couscous Salad with Roasted Butternut Squash

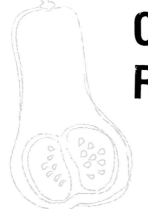

2 tbsp honey

4 tbsp olive oil

1 butternut squash, peeled,
   seeded, and cut into
   ¾-inch/2-cm chunks

generous 1¼ cups couscous

1¾ cups low-salt vegetable stock

½ cucumber, diced

1 zucchini, diced

1 red bell pepper, seeded
   and diced

juice of ½ lemon

2 tbsp chopped fresh parsley

sea salt and pepper

Preheat the oven to 375°F/190°C. Mix half the honey with 1 tablespoon of the oil in a large bowl, add the squash, and toss well to coat. Tip into a roasting pan and roast in the preheated oven for 30–40 minutes until soft and golden.

Meanwhile, put the couscous in a heatproof bowl. Heat the stock in a pan and pour over the couscous, cover, and leave for 3 minutes. Add 1 tablespoon of the remaining oil and fork through, then stir in the diced cucumber, zucchini, and red bell pepper. Re-cover and keep warm.

Whisk the remaining honey and oil with the lemon juice in a pitcher and season to taste with salt and pepper. Stir the mixture through the couscous.

To serve, top the couscous with the roasted squash and sprinkle with the parsley.

Serves 4

Creamy Pasta Bake

Preheat the oven to 375°F/190°C. Cook the whole wheat pasta in a large pan of boiling water for 10–12 minutes until just tender, then drain.

Meanwhile, heat the oil in a large skillet and cook the mushrooms until beginning to brown. Boil or steam the broccoli until just cooked, then drain.

Add the chicken to the mushrooms and stir well. Blend the cornstarch with a little milk in a pitcher, then gradually add the remaining milk, stirring. Pour into the pan, add the sour cream, and warm through, stirring.

Add the pasta and broccoli to the skillet and season to taste with salt and pepper. Mix well, then transfer to a baking dish, top with the cheese, and bake in the preheated oven for 15 minutes. Serve hot.

6 oz/175 g whole wheat pasta
  shells
1 tbsp olive oil
4½ oz/125 g white mushrooms,
  quartered
1 broccoli crown, broken into
  small florets
2 cooked skinless, boneless
  chicken breasts, shredded
1 tbsp cornstarch
scant 1 cup milk
½ cup half-fat sour cream
1¾ oz/50 g Cheddar cheese, grated
sea salt and pepper

Preparing healthy party food may be the biggest culinary challenge of all for parents. The combination of excitement, friends, gifts, and sugar overload has led to many a party meltdown. Most traditional party foods are fairly unhealthy, and while you don't want to deprive your child of treats, there are fun ways to make healthy foods appealing for the partygoers.

4 party

This chapter offers a variety of appetizing and delicious foods that work well at parties and even includes a healthy birthday cake that is nevertheless attractive. Children tend to like finger food at parties and want a colorful and tempting choice of items, so offer a good range of bite-size morsels, and the right balance of savory and sweet foods. Offer only the savory options at first and bring out the sweet ones after the kids have eaten at least some of the savory. Try starting the party off by giving each child an individual party box, labeled with his or her name, which contains a selection of finger foods, such as a cocktail frank, chicken drumstick, mini quiche, a couple of pinwheel sandwiches, and a savory straw. Kids can have these before sitting down at the table for the sweet treats. Fruit cocktails or smoothies decorated with umbrellas and fresh fruit are entertaining and a healthy party substitute for sodas. If you offer sandwiches, make them fingers, pinwheels, or in novelty shapes to encourage the kids to try them. Use as many healthy fillings as possible.

Presentation is important in tempting children to eat, so think carefully about this aspect of party food. Use colorful paper plates, napkins, and tablecloths, and consider choosing an imaginative theme to bring all the elements together.

Honey Sesame Sausages

1 tbsp olive oil, plus extra
    for oiling
2 tbsp honey
24 lean organic cocktail pork
    sausages (franks)
2 tbsp sesame seeds

Preheat the oven to 375°F/190°C. Brush a nonstick baking sheet with a little oil and place in the oven.

Whisk the honey and oil together in a large bowl, add the sausages, and toss well to coat.

Spread the sesame seeds out on a large piece of waxed paper and roll each sausage in the seeds until well coated.

Remove the baking sheet from the oven and place the sausages on it. Bake the sausages in the preheated oven for 10 minutes. Turn the sausages over and bake for an additional 10–15 minutes until well browned and sticky.

Serve warm or cold, either on sticks or in individual bowls.

Makes 12

Mini Crunchy Banana Sandwiches

Preheat the oven to 375°F/190°C. Mix the butter and cinnamon together in a bowl until well combined. Spread sparingly on both sides of the bread.

Using novelty cookie cutters, cut out fun shapes from the bread slices, such as stars, moons, and so on.

Place the shapes on a baking sheet and bake in the preheated oven for 8–10 minutes until golden. Remove from the oven and let cool.

Just before serving, mix the banana and chocolate together and use to sandwich the shapes together.

7 tbsp unsalted butter, softened
1 teaspoon ground cinnamon
6 slices whole wheat bread
1 large, ripe banana, thinly sliced
1 oz/25 g semisweet chocolate
   (minimum 70% cocoa solids),
   shaved

Sticky Drumsticks
with Cucumber Salad

6 organic chicken drumsticks

2 tbsp maple syrup

2 tbsp low-salt soy sauce

1 tsp sesame oil

½ cucumber, thinly sliced

2 scallions, thinly sliced

sea salt

Preheat the oven to 375°F/190°C. Trim the chicken drumsticks of any excess skin and pat dry with paper towels.

Mix the maple syrup, soy sauce, and sesame oil in a large bowl. Add the chicken drumsticks and toss well to coat.

Place the chicken drumsticks on a nonstick baking sheet and roast in the preheated oven for 30–40 minutes, basting occasionally, until the chicken is tender, well browned and sticky, and the juices run clear when a skewer is inserted into the thickest part of the meat.

Meanwhile, put the cucumber in a colander and sprinkle with a little salt. Leave for 10 minutes until the juices have drained out. Pat dry with paper towels and mix with the scallions.

Serve the chicken hot or cold with the cucumber salad.

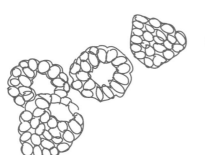

Very Berry Dessert

1 x ½-oz/12-g sachet of sugar-free
    raspberry or strawberry gelatine
scant 1 cup unsweetened
    cranberry juice
1 lb 2 oz/500 g raspberries,
    strawberries, red currants,
    blueberries, and blackberries

Make up the gelatine according to the package directions, but use the cranberry juice to replace some of the water.

Place a mixture of berries in the bottom of individual serving glasses or plastic cups and pour over the gelatine. Let chill for 6 hours until firmly set.

Serve decorated with more berries.

Serves 6–8

Avocado Dip with Spicy Potato Skins

Preheat the oven to 375°F/190°C. Rub the potatoes with 1 tablespoon of the oil, place on a baking sheet. and bake in the preheated oven for 1–1½ hours until the flesh is soft.

Remove the potatoes from the oven, cut in half lengthwise, and carefully scoop out the flesh into a bowl, but leave a generous ½ inch/1 cm of the potato on the skins. Set aside the potato flesh for the dip.

Cut the skins into wedges. Put the remaining oil in a large bowl with the garlic, paprika, and red pepper flakes and mix until combined. Season sparingly with salt and pepper.

Toss the potato wedges in the spicy oil, spread out on the baking sheet, and bake in the oven for 20 minutes until the skins are brown and crisp.

Meanwhile, to make the dip, in a separate bowl mash the avocado with the lemon juice, then mash in the cheese and potato flesh until well combined and smooth.

Serve the spicy skins warm, piled up, with little pots of the dip.

4 large baking potatoes, scrubbed
3 tbsp olive oil
1 garlic clove, crushed
¼ tsp paprika
½ tsp dried red pepper flakes
    (optional)
2 ripe avocados, pitted and peeled
juice of ½ lemon
5½ oz/150 g soft goat cheese
sea salt and pepper

12 slices

Party Carrot Cake

Preheat the oven to 350°F/180°C. Grease and line an 8-inch/20-cm round cake pan.

Mix the flours, baking powder, salt, and spices together in a large bowl and stir in the sugar and walnuts. Add the bananas and carrots and mix well.

In a separate bowl, mix the oil, eggs, and vanilla extract together. Pour into the flour mixture and mix well to combine. Spoon the mixture into the prepared cake pan and level the surface.

Bake in the preheated oven for 1 hour, then test to see if it is cooked by inserting a skewer into the center. If it comes out clean, the cake is done. If not, bake for an additional 10 minutes and test again. Remove from the oven and let cool in the pan.

Turn the cake out onto a serving plate and spread with the cream cheese, if using. To make mini "carrots" for decoration, cut each apricot in half horizontally and cut the snake into 12 1¼-inch/3-cm lengths. Use 2 pieces of the snake to form the carrot "stem" and roll an apricot half around it to form a mini carrot. Repeat until you have 6 "carrots." Use to decorate the cake.

unsalted butter, for greasing
scant 1 cup light brown self-
    rising flour
scant ¾ cup white self-raising flour
2 tsp baking powder
pinch of sea salt
1 tsp ground cinnamon
1 tsp ground nutmeg
generous ⅛ cup raw brown sugar
generous ⅜ cup shelled walnuts,
    chopped
2 ripe bananas, peeled and mashed
3½ oz/100 g carrots, peeled and
    finely grated
⅔ cup light sunflower oil
2 eggs, beaten
1 tsp vanilla extract
cream cheese (optional)
3 no-soak dried apricots
green confectionery snake

Mini Quiches

Preheat the oven to 400°F/200°C. Lightly grease a 12-hole muffin pan with butter.

Put the flours, butter, and a pinch of salt in a food processor and pulse until the mixture resembles bread crumbs. Add the egg yolk and pulse again to form a dough, adding a little cold water if necessary. Alternatively, mix the flours and salt together in a large bowl, add the butter, and rub in with your fingertips until the mixture resembles bread crumbs. Mix in the egg yolk to form a dough, adding a little cold water if necessary. Turn out onto a floured counter and knead briefly. Divide the dough into 12 pieces, roll out each piece into a 4½-inch/12-cm circle, and use to line the muffin holes. Let chill for 30 minutes. Meanwhile, heat the oil in a pan over low heat and cook the leek and zucchini until soft.

Remove the muffin pan from the refrigerator and line each pastry shell with parchment paper and dried beans. Bake blind for 10 minutes, then lift out the paper and beans. Divide the vegetable mixture between the pastry shells, top with the ham, and sprinkle with the cheese.

Reduce the oven temperature to 350°F/180°C. Whisk 2 eggs with the milk in a bowl, season to taste with pepper, and pour into the pastry shells. Bake for 18–20 minutes until golden. Remove from the oven and let cool in the pan.

7 tbsp unsalted butter, diced and chilled, plus extra for greasing
scant 1 cup white all-purpose flour, plus extra for dusting
scant 1 cup whole wheat all-purpose flour
1 egg yolk
1 tbsp olive oil
1 leek, minced
1 zucchini, finely sliced
4 slices thin ham, chopped
1¾ oz/50 g Gruyère or Cheddar cheese, grated
2 large eggs
scant 1 cup whole milk
sea salt and pepper

Coconut Granola Squares

9 tbsp unsalted butter, softened, plus extra for greasing

generous ⅜ cup packed brown sugar

1 egg yolk

generous 1 cup whole wheat all-purpose flour

1 heaping tbsp no-added-sugar custard powder

6 tbsp honey

1½ cups rolled oats

generous ⅜ cup dry unsweetened coconut

2¾ oz/75 g dried mango, chopped

generous ⅛ cup shelled Brazil nuts, chopped

Preheat the oven to 375°F/190°C. Take an 8½-inch/ 22-cm square baking pan that is 1¼ inches/3 cm deep, and grease and line it.

Beat 7 tablespoons of the softened butter with the sugar and egg yolk, using an electric mixer, or by hand, until light and fluffy. Fold in the flour and custard powder and mix well. Spoon into the baking pan, level the surface, and bake in the preheated oven for 15 minutes.

Meanwhile, melt the remaining butter and 5 tablespoons of the honey in a small pan over low heat. Put the oats, coconut, mango, and nuts in a bowl, add the melted butter and honey, and stir to combine.

Remove the baking pan from the oven and spread the sponge with the remaining honey. Top with the coconut mixture and press down well. Return to the oven and bake for an additional 15 minutes.

Remove from the oven and let cool in the pan, then cut into 16 squares.

Makes 20

Tuna Bites

Mash the tuna with the egg, parsley, a pinch of salt, and pepper to taste. Add the bread crumbs and mix well, then add enough of the flour to bind the mixture together.

Divide the mixture into 20 mini portions, shape each portion into a ball, and let chill for 15 minutes.

Meanwhile, preheat the oven to 375°F/190°C. Brush a nonstick baking sheet with a little oil. Space the tuna balls out on the baking sheet and brush with a little more oil. Bake in the preheated oven for 15–20 minutes until golden and crisp.

Remove from the oven and drain on paper towels. Serve warm or cold.

7 oz/200 g canned tuna in spring
  water, drained
1 egg
1 tsp minced fresh parsley
scant 1 cup fresh whole wheat
  bread crumbs
about 1 tbsp whole wheat
  all-purpose flour
vegetable oil, for brushing
sea salt and pepper

Makes 10

Strawberry Cupcakes

Preheat the oven to 350°F/180°C. Line 10 holes of a muffin pan with paper cake cases.

Beat the butter with the sugars in a bowl until pale and fluffy, then beat in the vanilla extract. Add half the egg and beat well.

In a separate bowl, mix the flours and cinnamon together, then add half to the butter mixture and stir to combine. Add the remaining egg and flour mixture and stir to combine. Add the mashed strawberries and mix well.

Spoon the batter into the paper cases and bake in the preheated oven for 15 minutes. Remove from the oven and let cool on a wire rack.

Just before serving, spread thinly with the mascarpone cheese and top with a strawberry half or a whole wild strawberry.

9 tbsp unsalted butter, softened

generous ⅜ cup unrefined
   superfine sugar

¼ cup packed raw brown sugar

1 tsp vanilla extract

2 large eggs, beaten

generous ½ cup white
   self-rising flour

generous ⅓ cup light brown
   self-rising flour

½ tsp ground cinnamon

2 large strawberries, mashed

5 strawberries, halved, or
   10 whole wild strawberries

3 tbsp mascarpone cheese

Pinwheel Sandwiches

finely mashed canned tuna
and mayonnaise

cream cheese and minced
wafer-thin ham

finely mashed egg and mayonnaise

goat cheese and mashed avocado
(add a little lemon juice to
prevent avocado discoloring)

grated cheese

mashed canned sardines and
cream cheese

thinly sliced cooked turkey
with cranberry sauce

no-added-sugar or -salt peanut
butter or other nut butters

Swiss cheese and chutney

ricotta cheese and honey

hummus

These are great party sandwiches, because kids like their shape and size and the fact that they don't look like normal sandwiches. Using whole wheat bread is the healthy option.

To make 6 pinwheels, you will need 1 slice of bread, with the crusts removed, plus the filling. Mash the filling with a little softened butter and spread over the bread. Starting with the short end, tightly roll up into a sausage shape. Repeat with more slices of bread and then let chill for 15–20 minutes. Remove from the refrigerator and, using a sharp knife, cut each "sausage" into 6 slices. To make the pinwheels neat and appealing, avoid using chunky fillings. Choose from the healthy fillings shown here.

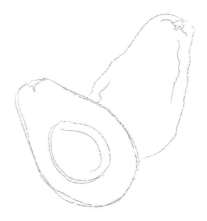

Cheese Star Cookies

Beat the butter with the cheeses in a bowl until well combined. Add the flours and salt and stir to combine. Mix in the egg yolk and oil to form a soft dough. Wrap the dough in plastic wrap and let chill for 30 minutes.

Meanwhile, preheat the oven to 350°F/180°C.

Remove the dough from the refrigerator, unwrap it, and roll it out on a floured counter. Using a star-shaped pastry cutter, cut out 35 stars, rerolling the trimmings where possible.

Place the cookies on a nonstick baking sheet, brush with the milk, and sprinkle over the seeds. Bake for 12–15 minutes until golden. Remove and let cool on a wire rack.

11 tbsp butter, softened

6 oz/175 g Parmesan cheese, finely grated

1¾ oz/50 g sharp Cheddar cheese, finely grated

scant ¾ cup all-purpose flour, plus extra for dusting

generous ⅔ cup whole wheat all-purpose flour

pinch of celery salt or sea salt

1 egg yolk

1 tbsp olive oil

2 tbsp whole milk

⅛ cup sesame seeds or flax seeds

Party Straws

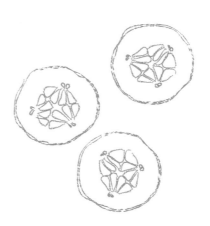

Use brightly colored straws rather than sticks to thread inviting and colorful morsels of food—each child could have 2 or 3 straws in a cup and perhaps offer an accompanying dip such as guacamole. You can make both savory and sweet straws, and obviously the more variety there is the better. Use a metal skewer to make a hole in each piece of food and thread onto the straws. Try the suggestions listed here or use your child's favorite foods.

Savory Straws
rolled up strips of cooked chicken, turkey, ham, salami, or pastrami
cherry tomatoes
radishes
cubes of hard cheese
individual mozzarella cheese balls
cooked lean organic sausage
mini gherkins, halved
baby corn
baby carrots, halved
squares of Spanish omelet
cooked chicken breast, cubed
silver skin onions (cocktail onions)

Sweet Straws
whole raspberries
halved or whole strawberries
chunks of banana, pineapple, mango, or papaya
kiwifruit or melon, cubed
dried fruit, cut into bite-size pieces
pitted cherries
seedless grapes
mandarin segments
pitted litchis

With increasingly hectic lives, it is sometimes difficult to assemble the family together for a meal. However, it is very important for kids to eat with the family, not only to develop their social skills, but also to learn by example—if you are eating healthily, it is far more likely that your children will do so. It is equally important to offer children a wide range of foods and encourage them to try new ones. Growing children need a good balance of all the food groups, and it is particularly vital to include as wide a variety as possible of fruit and vegetables for optimum vitamin and mineral intake, as well as "good" fats and oils. No food should be off-limits, but those high in saturated fats, sugar, and salt should not feature heavily in your child's diet. And remember to avoid falling into the trap of using food as a bribe, because this places an emphasis and importance on certain foods—usually the unhealthy ones! It is crucial that kids don't develop the idea that some foods are more important or desirable than others.

5 family meals

Eating healthily will benefit everyone and the recipes in this chapter offer an opportunity for all the family to enjoy good, nutritious food. There are some straightforward ways to improve the nutritional value of certain foods by simply adapting them—for instance, if your kids love pasta, make a Roast Vegetable Lasagna with five or six different vegetables instead of meat. Try to add vegetables whenever possible and use beans to bulk up traditionally meat-based recipes. Vary the types of foods you prepare throughout the week for maximum nutritional benefit and to maintain your child's interest in food and cooking.

Easy Biscuit Pizzas

2 tbsp olive oil, plus extra
    for oiling

1 onion, chopped

1 lb 12 oz/800 g canned chopped
    tomatoes, drained

1 tsp tomato paste

1 tbsp fresh thyme leaves

1 red bell pepper, seeded and
    thinly sliced

1 yellow bell pepper, seeded and
    thinly sliced

1 zucchini, thinly sliced

5⅝ cups baby spinach leaves

1¾ cups whole wheat
    all-purpose flour

generous 1¼ cups white
    all-purpose flour, plus extra
    for dusting

1 tsp raw brown sugar

1 tsp baking soda

1 tsp sea salt

1½ cups buttermilk

3 slices ham, chopped

9 oz/250 g mozzarella,
    thinly sliced

pepper

Heat half the oil in a large skillet and cook the onion for 5 minutes until soft but not browned. Add the tomatoes, tomato paste, and thyme and season to taste with pepper. Let simmer for 30 minutes until you have a thick sauce with almost no liquid. Remove from the skillet and let cool.

Heat the remaining oil in the skillet and cook the bell peppers and zucchini for 5–8 minutes until just beginning to brown. Let cool.

Put the spinach in a colander and pour boiling water from a kettle over the leaves to wilt. Let cool, then squeeze all the liquid out until the spinach is very dry. Mince.

Preheat the oven to 425°F/220°C. Lightly oil 2 baking sheets. Put the flours, sugar, baking soda, and salt in a large bowl, add the buttermilk, and mix well to form a dough. Turn out onto a floured counter and knead briefly.

Divide the dough into 6 pieces, roll out each piece into a 5-inch/13-cm circle and place on the prepared baking sheets. Spread the pizza bases with the tomato sauce, then top with the spinach, bell peppers, zucchini, ham, and cheese. Bake in the preheated oven for 25 minutes.

Remove from the oven and serve.

Burritos

1 tbsp olive oil

1 onion, chopped

1 garlic clove, minced

1 lb 2 oz/500 g extra-lean fresh
    ground beef

3 large tomatoes, seeded and
    chopped

1 red bell pepper, seeded and
    chopped

½ red chili, minced (optional)

14 oz/400 g canned no-added-salt
    mixed beans, drained

14 oz/400 g canned no-added-salt
    red kidney beans, drained

½ cup low-salt vegetable stock

1 tbsp minced fresh parsley

8 whole wheat flour tortillas

½ cup strained canned tomatoes

1¾ oz/50 g Cheddar cheese, grated

3 scallions, sliced

sea salt and pepper

mixed salad, to serve

Heat the oil in a large, nonstick skillet and cook the onion and garlic until the onion is soft but not browned. Remove from the skillet with a slotted spoon. Add the ground beef and cook over high heat, breaking up with a wooden spoon, for 3–4 minutes until beginning to brown. Drain off any excess oil.

Return the onion and garlic to the skillet, add the tomatoes and red bell pepper, and chili if using, and cook for 8–10 minutes. Add the mixed beans, kidney beans, stock, and parsley, season to taste with salt and pepper, and cook, uncovered, for an additional 20–30 minutes until well thickened. Meanwhile, preheat the oven to 350°F/180°C.

Mash the meat mixture to break up the beans, then divide between the tortillas. Roll each one up and place, seam-side down, in a baking dish.

Pour the strained canned tomatoes over the burritos and sprinkle over the cheese. Bake in the preheated oven for 20 minutes. Remove from the oven, sprinkle over the scallions, and serve with a mixed salad.

Makes 12

Salmon Fishcakes

Preheat the oven to 400°F/200°C. Put the salmon in a pan with the milk and bay leaf and bring slowly up to simmering point. Let simmer for 2 minutes, then remove the pan from the heat, lift out and discard the bay leaf, and leave the fish in the milk to cool. When cool, lift out the fish with a slotted spoon onto paper towels to drain.

Flake the fish into a large bowl. Put the broccoli in a food processor and pulse until smooth. Add to the fish with the mashed potatoes, the parsley, 1 tablespoon of the flour, and pepper to taste. Add the egg yolk and mix well. If the mixture is a little dry, add some of the poaching milk; if too wet, add a little more flour.

Divide the mixture into 12 portions and shape each portion into a cake. Put the beaten eggs, remaining flour, and the bread crumbs on 3 separate plates. Roll each fishcake in the flour, then in the beaten egg, and then in the bread crumbs to coat.

Heat the oil in a nonstick baking sheet with a rim in the preheated oven for 5 minutes. Add the fishcakes and bake for 10 minutes, then carefully turn the fishcakes over and bake for an additional 10 minutes.

1 lb 9 oz/700 g skinless salmon
   fillet, cut into cubes
1¼ cups whole milk
1 bay leaf
3½ oz/100 g broccoli, steamed
   until tender
1 lb 9 oz/700 g potatoes, boiled
   and mashed
2 tbsp minced fresh parsley
4 tbsp whole wheat
   all-purpose flour
1 egg yolk
2 large eggs, beaten
2¾ cups fresh whole wheat
   bread crumbs
2 tbsp olive oil
pepper

Sweet Potato, Cheese, and Leek Pie

2 tbsp olive oil

2 garlic cloves, minced

scant 1 cup sour cream

3 lb/1.3 kg sweet potatoes, peeled and thinly sliced

1 tsp butter, plus extra for greasing

2 leeks, finely sliced

2¾ oz/75 g Gruyère cheese, grated

½ cup fresh whole wheat bread crumbs

pepper

Preheat the oven to 375°F/190°C. Mix the oil, garlic, and sour cream together in a large bowl, add the sweet potato slices, and toss until well coated.

Melt the butter in a nonstick skillet and cook the leeks until soft. Add to the sweet potatoes and mix until evenly distributed. Season to taste with pepper.

Lightly grease a gratin dish. Layer in the sweet potato mixture and top with the cheese and bread crumbs.

Cover with foil and bake in the preheated oven for 1 hour, removing the foil for the last 5 minutes of the cooking time.

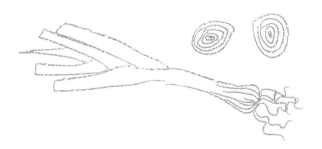

Serves 4

Sausage and Bean Casserole

Preheat the oven to 350°F/180°C. Heat the oil in a nonstick skillet and briefly brown the sausages. Remove from the pan with a slotted spoon and drain on paper towels. Add the onion and red bell pepper to the skillet and cook until soft, then add the tomatoes and let simmer for an additional 2–3 minutes.

Add the mixed beans, strained canned tomatoes, parsley, and tomato paste, and salt and pepper to taste, and cook for 5 minutes.

Spoon the mixed beans and sauce into a casserole dish and add the sausages. Cover and cook in the preheated oven for 25 minutes.

Remove from the oven and serve hot with a swirl of yogurt.

1 tbsp olive oil

8 lean organic pork sausages

1 onion, minced

1 red bell pepper, seeded and
   chopped

6 tomatoes, seeded and chopped

2 lb 10 oz/1.2 kg canned no-salt-
   added mixed beans, drained

2½ cups strained canned tomatoes

1 tbsp chopped fresh parsley

1 tbsp tomato paste

3 tbsp plain yogurt

sea salt and pepper

Serves 4

Mashed Potato and Hamburger Casserole

Heat half the oil in a nonstick skillet and cook the ground lamb over high heat, breaking up with a wooden spoon, until well browned. Remove the ground lamb from the skillet with a slotted spoon, pour away any fat, and wipe the skillet with paper towels.

Add the remaining oil to the skillet and cook the leek, onion, carrots, and celery for 15 minutes until soft. Return the lamb to the pan and add the mushrooms, tomatoes, thyme, and water. Season to taste with salt and pepper and let simmer for 40 minutes, stirring occasionally.

Meanwhile, preheat the oven to 350°F/180°C. Mix the 2 mashes of potatoes with half the milk and half the butter in a bowl and season to taste with salt and pepper.

Spoon the meat sauce into a baking dish and top with the potato mixture. Brush with the remaining milk and dot with the remaining butter. Bake in the preheated oven for 35 minutes until the topping is brown and crisp.

2 tbsp olive oil
1 lb 10 oz/750 g lean fresh
    ground lamb or beef
1 leek, chopped
1 small red onion, chopped
2 carrots, chopped
1 celery stalk, chopped
3½ oz/100 g mushrooms, chopped
14 oz/400 g canned tomatoes
2 tbsp fresh thyme leaves
½ cup water
1 lb 2 oz/500 g potatoes,
    boiled and mashed
14 oz/400 g sweet potatoes,
    boiled and mashed
4 tbsp whole milk
piece of unsalted butter
sea salt and pepper

Roast Vegetable Lasagna

3 tbsp olive oil

4 zucchini, halved lengthwise
   and thickly sliced

3 red bell peppers, seeded and
   chopped

1 eggplant, chopped

2 red onions, chopped

5 shallots, peeled and quartered

9 oz/250 g white mushrooms

14 oz/400 g canned chopped
   tomatoes

1 tbsp tomato paste

3½ tbsp butter

generous ⅓ cup all-purpose flour
   or gluten-free flour

2½ cups whole milk

3½ oz/100 g Cheddar cheese,
   grated

7 oz/200 g fresh lasagna noodles

2 tbsp grated Parmesan cheese

sea salt and pepper

salad greens, to serve

Preheat the oven to 375°F/190°C. Put the oil in a large bowl, add the zucchini, bell peppers, eggplant, onions, and shallots and toss well to coat.

Divide the vegetables between 2 baking sheets and roast in the preheated oven for 30–40 minutes until soft and flecked with brown. Add the white mushrooms after 20 minutes.

Remove the vegetables from the oven and tip into a large bowl. Add the tomatoes and tomato paste and mix well.

Melt the butter in a pan over low heat. Stir in the flour and cook, stirring constantly, for 2–3 minutes. Gradually add the milk and cook, continuing to stir constantly, until the sauce is thick and smooth. Season to taste with salt and pepper and stir in the Cheddar cheese.

Layer the vegetable mixture and sauce in an ovenproof dish with the lasagna, finishing with a layer of sauce. Sprinkle over the Parmesan cheese and bake in the oven for 30–35 minutes.

Remove from the oven and serve hot with a green salad.

Roasted Chicken and Sweet Potatoes

8 organic chicken thighs, skinned

1 red onion, minced

8 tbsp low-sugar and -salt tomato
    ketchup

2 tbsp maple syrup

1 tbsp Worcestershire sauce

1 tbsp coarse grain mustard

1 garlic clove, minced

3 tbsp olive oil

4 sweet potatoes, cut into chunks

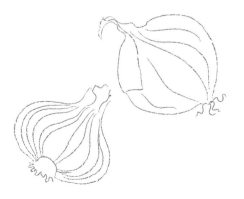

Preheat the oven to 400°F/200°C. Score each chicken
thigh 2–3 times.

Mix all the remaining ingredients, except the sweet
potatoes, together in a large bowl. Add the chicken and
toss well to coat. Cover with plastic wrap and let marinate
in a cool place for 20 minutes, then add the sweet
potatoes and toss well to coat.

Tip the chicken and sweet potatoes into a baking dish and
roast in the preheated oven for 40–50 minutes until well
browned. The chicken should be tender and the juices
run clear when a skewer is inserted into the thickest part
of the meat.

The chicken thighs and sweet potatoes could also be
cooked on a barbecue in the summer.

Serves 4

Chicken and Leek Pie

Put the chicken, onion, carrot, celery, and herbs in an ovenproof casserole and cover with cold water. Cover and bring to a boil, then reduce the heat and let simmer for 1 hour, or until the chicken is tender and the juices run clear when a skewer is inserted into the thickest part of the meat. Remove the chicken from the casserole. Discard the skin. Remove the meat from the carcass, cut into chunks and set aside. Strain the chicken cooking liquid, discarding the vegetables and herbs, and set aside.

Preheat the oven to 375°F/190°C. Heat the oil in a large skillet and cook the onion until soft but not browned. Remove from the skillet with a slotted spoon and set aside. Melt the butter in the skillet and cook the leeks for 5 minutes. Stir in the flour and cook, stirring constantly, for 2–3 minutes. Gradually add scant 2 cups of the reserved cooking liquid and cook, continuing to stir constantly, until the sauce is thick and smooth. Stir in the mushrooms and ham. Mix the cooked chicken with the onion and the sauce and stir in the cream. Season to taste with salt and pepper and spoon into a baking dish.

Brush each sheet of phyllo pastry with a little of the vegetable oil, then scrunch up and place over the chicken mixture. Bake in the preheated oven for 30 minutes until the phyllo pastry topping is brown and crisp.

1 organic chicken, weighing
   3 lb/1.3 kg
1 onion, quartered
1 carrot, cut into chunks
1 celery stalk, cut into chunks
1 bay leaf
1 fresh rosemary sprig
3 tbsp olive oil
1 red onion, chopped
2 tbsp butter
3 leeks, sliced
scant ¼ cup all-purpose or
   gluten-free flour
9 oz/250 g portobello or cremini
   mushrooms, halved
3½ oz/100 g ham, sliced
3 tbsp heavy cream
4 sheets phyllo pastry, thawed
   if frozen
2 tbsp vegetable oil
sea salt and pepper

Makes 12 slices

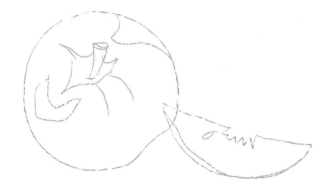

Apple Cake

Preheat the oven to 350°F/180°C. Grease and line a 9-inch/23-cm round cake pan. Arrange the apple slices in the bottom of the prepared pan.

Put all the remaining ingredients, except the honey and dried apple, in a food processor and pulse until well combined. Pour the cake batter over the apples and bake in the preheated oven for 1 hour until cooked through—a skewer inserted into the center of the cake should come out clean.

Remove from the oven and let cool in the pan, then invert onto a plate and remove the lining paper. Turn back over onto a serving plate. Spread the top of the cake with the honey and sprinkle over the dried apple. Cut into 12 equal pieces.

1 cup/2 sticks unsalted butter, diced, plus extra for greasing
3 apples, peeled, cored, and sliced
½ cup unrefined superfine sugar
½ cup packed raw brown sugar
½ tsp vanilla extract
½ tsp ground cinnamon
4 large eggs
scant ¾ cup light brown self-rising flour
scant 1 cup white self-rising flour
1 tsp baking powder
1 tbsp honey
3–4 slices dried apple, chopped

Raspberry Fool

2⅜ cups fresh raspberries, plus extra to decorate

1 cup plain or strained plain yogurt

1 tbsp honey

1 egg white

generous ⅜ cup toasted slivered almonds

Put the raspberries in a blender or food processor and process until smooth. Pour the purée through a fine nylon strainer to remove the seeds, then fold into the yogurt in a large bowl. Stir in the honey.

In a separate grease-free bowl, whisk the egg white until beginning to stiffen, then fold into the raspberry mixture.

Spoon into individual glasses, cover with plastic wrap, and let chill for 3 hours. Sprinkle over the almonds and the extra fresh raspberries before serving.

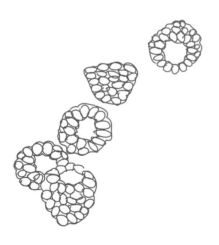

Serves 4

Plum Crisp

Preheat the oven to 350°F/180°C. Arrange the plums in the bottom of a baking dish.

Put the oats, almonds, nuts, honey, and sugar in a bowl. Melt the butter in a small pan over low heat, pour into the oat mixture, and stir to combine. Spoon over the plums. Bake in the preheated oven for 35 minutes.

Remove the dish from the oven and serve hot with strained plain yogurt.

1 lb 10 oz/750 g ripe plums,
    pitted and halved
scant 1 cup jumbo oats
generous ⅜ cup slivered almonds
generous ⅓ cup shelled pecans,
    chopped
4 tbsp honey
2 tbsp raw brown sugar
3½ tbsp unsalted butter
strained plain yogurt, to serve

Crispy Vegetable Bake

Preheat the oven to 375°F/190°C. Grease an 8-inch/20-cm round baking dish with butter.

Cook the potato slices in a large pan of boiling water for 5 minutes. Drain and cover with a clean dish towel to absorb the steam.

Melt half the butter with 1 tablespoon of the oil in a large skillet and cook the garlic, oregano, and leek for 3–4 minutes. Remove with a slotted spoon and transfer to a plate. Add the remaining oil to the skillet and cook the parsnips, carrots, and celery root for 10 minutes until soft and cooked through. Season to taste with salt and pepper and cook for another 5 minutes. Stir in the leek mixture.

Arrange half the potato slices in the bottom of the prepared dish, top with half the vegetable mixture, and then sprinkle over half the cheese. Cover with the remaining vegetable mixture and cheese and top with the remaining potato slices. Dot with the remaining butter and bake in the preheated oven for 40 minutes until golden and crisp.

Five minutes before serving, poach the eggs. Serve the vegetable bake topped with the poached eggs, accompanied by a green salad.

2 tbsp butter, plus extra
   for greasing
1 lb 10 oz/750 g potatoes,
   thinly sliced
3 tbsp olive oil
1 garlic clove, crushed
1 tsp fresh oregano leaves
1 large leek, shredded
2 parsnips, peeled and grated
3 carrots, peeled and grated
½ head celery root, peeled
   and grated
7 oz/200 g feta cheese, crumbled
4 eggs
sea salt and pepper
green salad, to serve

Winter Fruit and Nut Crumble

Preheat the oven to 375°F/190°C. Put the apples in a pan with the water and 1 tablespoon of the honey over medium heat. Cook for 10 minutes. Let cool, then mix with the blackberries. Arrange the fruit mixture in the bottom of a baking dish.

Melt the butter in a small pan over low heat. Let cool slightly. Meanwhile, mix all the remaining ingredients together in a large bowl. Pour in the melted butter and stir to combine. Spoon over the fruit mixture in the dish.

Bake in the preheated oven for 35–40 minutes. Serve hot with half-fat cream cheese.

3 lb/1.3 kg cooking apples, peeled,
    cored, and chopped, or a
    mixture of apples and quinces
1 tbsp water
3 tbsp honey
1¾ cups blackberries
2 tbsp unsalted butter
2 tbsp raw brown sugar
3 tbsp whole wheat
    all-purpose flour
2⅓ cups rolled oats
1 tsp ground nutmeg
2 tbsp toasted hazelnuts, chopped
half-fat cream cheese, to serve

Serves 4

Banana Cinnamon Bread and Butter Pudding

Preheat the oven to 350°F/180°C. Lightly grease a baking dish and arrange the banana slices in the bottom. Top with the bread slices, overlapping each slice to cover the banana.

Whisk the sugar, eggs, milk, and cinnamon together in a bowl and pour over the bread.

Drizzle over the honey and bake in the preheated oven for 30–40 minutes until risen and golden.

unsalted butter, for greasing

2 bananas, peeled and sliced

8 slices malted whole grain bread, lightly buttered and cut in half diagonally, crusts removed

2 tbsp raw brown sugar

3 large eggs

1¼ cups whole milk

1½ tsp ground cinnamon

2 tbsp honey

A great way to develop your children's positive interest in food is to involve them, when you can, in preparing and cooking it, and no matter how young they are, there is invariably some way in which they can participate. It takes very little effort to introduce children to the basics of good food, and they are much more likely to try a dish if they have been involved in making it than if it simply appears on a plate in front of them. This chapter offers recipes that are not only fun for children to help you make, but are really delicious to eat and healthy, too.

6 treats

Needless to say, it is virtually impossible to insulate children against the might of the fast-food giants, but if they really do want burgers and chicken nuggets, then make them bean burgers and homemade nuggets. You can usually find a way of making healthier, homemade versions of fast-food menu items. Chocolate is another obvious pull for kids, but as no food should be off-limits, find ways of including it in a limited way and in conjunction with some fruit, because this is a good source of antioxidants, and choose chocolate with a high proportion of cocoa solids (70%).

Many of the processed foods that children ask for are packaged in bright colors and feature cartoon characters—all specially designed to attract kids. But you can use the same techniques to encourage your child to choose the healthy option. Chop fruit and vegetables into fun shapes and utilize novelty cookie cutters. Serve food on paper plates showing their favorite cartoon characters, and present healthy snacks in unusual ways, such as chopped fruit and nuts in little pots or mini boxes. Make healthy food a treat through the variety and originality of its presentation.

Spicy Bean Burgers

Mash the beans with a potato masher in a bowl until they are smooth, then add the pesto, bread crumbs, egg, a pinch of salt, and pepper to taste, and mix well.

14 oz/400 g canned cannellini
   beans, drained and rinsed
2 tbsp red pesto
1⅜ cups fresh whole wheat
   bread crumbs
1 egg
2 tbsp olive oil
½ small red onion, minced
1 garlic clove, crushed
6 whole wheat rolls
6 tsp hummus
pepper
sea salt

To serve
6 cherry tomatoes, sliced
sliced cucumber or cornichons
salad greens

Heat half the oil in a nonstick skillet over low heat and cook the onion and garlic until soft. Add to the bean mixture and mix well.

Heat the remaining oil in the skillet. Spoon in the bean mixture, in 6 separate mounds, then press each one down with the back of a spoon to form a burger.

Cook the burgers for 4–5 minutes, then carefully turn over and cook for an additional 4–5 minutes until golden.

Meanwhile, slice the rolls in half and smear each one with the hummus.

Remove the burgers from the skillet and drain on paper towels. Place each one in a roll, top with the tomatoes, cucumber, and salad greens, and serve.

Serves 4

Chicken Nuggets

Preheat the oven to 375°F/190°C. Cut the chicken breasts into 1½-inch/4-cm chunks. Mix the flour, wheat germ, cumin, coriander, and pepper to taste, in a bowl, then divide in half and put on 2 separate plates. Put the beaten egg on a third plate.

Pour the oil into a baking sheet with a rim and heat in the oven. Roll the chicken pieces in one plate of flour, shake to remove any excess, then roll in the egg and in the second plate of flour, again shaking off any excess flour. When all the nuggets are ready, remove the baking sheet from the oven and toss the nuggets in the hot oil. Roast in the oven for 25–30 minutes until golden and crisp.

Meanwhile, to make the dipping sauce, put both kinds of tomatoes in a blender or food processor and process until smooth. Add the mayonnaise and process again until well combined.

Remove the nuggets from the oven and drain on paper towels. Serve with the dipping sauce and a green salad.

3 organic skinless, boneless
    chicken breasts
4 tbsp whole wheat
    all-purpose flour
1 tbsp wheat germ
½ tsp ground cumin
½ tsp ground coriander
1 egg, lightly beaten
2 tbsp olive oil
3½ oz/100 g sunblush tomatoes
3½ oz/100 g fresh tomatoes,
    peeled, seeded, and chopped
2 tbsp mayonnaise
pepper
green salad, to serve

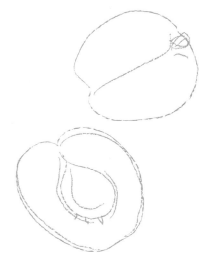

Fruit Skewers

Soak 4 bamboo skewers in water for at least 20 minutes.

Preheat the broiler to high and line the broiler pan with foil. Thread alternate pieces of fruit onto each skewer. Brush the fruit with a little maple syrup.

selection of fruit, such as apricots, peaches, figs, strawberries, mangoes, pineapple, bananas, dates, and papaya, prepared and cut into chunks
maple syrup
1¾ oz/50 g semisweet chocolate (minimum 70% cocoa solids), broken into chunks

Put the chocolate in a heatproof bowl, set the bowl over a pan of barely simmering water, and heat until it is melted.

Meanwhile, cook the skewers under the preheated broiler for 3 minutes, or until caramelized. Serve drizzled with a little of the melted chocolate, removing the fruit from the skewer if serving to younger children.

Makes 6

Cherry Rascals

Preheat the oven to 375°F/190°C. Put the flours, baking powder, and butter in a food processor and pulse until the mixture resembles bread crumbs. Add the sugar, lemon rind, spices, and cherries and pulse briefly to mix. Add the egg and milk and pulse again to form a soft dough. Alternatively, mix the flours and baking powder together in a large bowl, add the butter and rub in with your fingertips until the mixture resembles bread crumbs. Stir in the sugar, lemon rind, spices, and cherries, then mix in the egg and milk to form a soft dough. Turn out onto a floured counter and knead briefly.

Divide the dough into 6 pieces, form each piece into a ball, and place on a baking sheet. Press down lightly, brush with milk and sprinkle with the nuts. Bake in the preheated oven for 15 minutes until golden.

Remove from the oven and let cool on a wire rack. Serve warm or cold.

generous ½ cup all-purpose flour, plus extra for dusting
generous ½ cup light brown self-rising flour
½ tsp baking powder
3½ tbsp unsalted butter, diced and chilled
¼ cup packed raw brown sugar
finely grated rind of 1 lemon
½ tsp ground cinnamon
½ tsp ground nutmeg
2¾ oz/75 g dried cherries
1 egg, beaten
2 tbsp whole milk, plus extra for brushing
2 tbsp chopped Brazil nuts

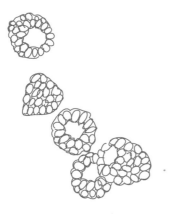

Yogurt Lollipops

Put the berries in a blender or food processor and pulse briefly to break them up. Add the yogurt and honey and process to combine.

Pour into 6 ¼ cup lollipop molds or plastic cups and insert a lollipop stick into each. Freeze for 6 hours.

To unmold, wrap each mold in a hot cloth and carefully lift out the lollipop.

generous 2 cups frozen mixed
    berries
1¾ cups whole plain yogurt
1 tbsp honey

Makes 12 slices

Cranberry and Pecan Slices

Preheat the oven to 350°F/180°C. Grease and line an 8½-inch/22-cm square baking pan.

Mix the granola, cranberries, nuts, and sugar together in a large bowl.

Warm the honey in a pan over low heat, then stir into the granola mixture. Stir in the egg whites and apple juice and mix well.

Spoon into the prepared baking pan and press down firmly. Bake in the preheated oven for 30 minutes.

Remove from the oven and let cool in the pan, then cut into 12 slices.

unsalted butter, for greasing
1⅝ cups no-added-sugar granola
generous ½ cup dried cranberries
generous ⅓ cup shelled pecans,
    chopped
¼ cup packed raw brown sugar
3 tbsp honey
2 egg whites, lightly beaten
¾ cup apple juice

Mini Strawberry Cheesecakes

5½ heaping tbsp unsalted butter
scant 1 cup rolled oats
generous ⅛ cup chopped hazelnuts
1 cup ricotta cheese
¼ cup packed raw brown sugar
finely grated rind of 1 lemon,
    and juice of ½ lemon
1 egg, plus 1 egg yolk
scant ¾ cup cottage cheese
1 kiwifruit
6 large strawberries

Line 6 holes of a muffin pan with muffin paper cases.

Melt the butter in a small pan over low heat, then let cool. Put the oats in a food processor and pulse briefly to break them up, then tip into a bowl, add the nuts, and melted butter and mix well. Divide the mixture between the paper cases and press down well. Let chill for 30 minutes.

Preheat the oven to 300°F/150°C. Beat the ricotta cheese with the sugar, and lemon rind and juice, in a bowl. Add the egg, egg yolk, and cottage cheese and mix well. Spoon into the muffin cases and bake in the preheated oven for 30 minutes. Turn off the oven, but leave the cheesecakes in the oven until completely cold.

Peel the kiwifruit and dice the flesh, and slice the strawberries. Remove the paper cases, top each cheesecake with the fruit, and serve.

Chocolate Mousse Pots

3½ oz/100 g semisweet chocolate
(minimum 70% cocoa solids),
chopped

1 tbsp butter

2 large eggs, separated

1 tbsp maple syrup

2 tbsp strained plain yogurt

⅝ cup blueberries

1 tbsp water

1 oz/25 g white chocolate, grated

Put the chocolate and butter in a heatproof bowl, set the bowl over a pan of barely simmering water, and heat until melted. Let cool slightly, then stir in the egg yolks, maple syrup, and yogurt.

Whisk the egg whites in a large, grease-free bowl until stiff, then fold into the chocolate mixture. Divide between 6 small pots or glasses and let chill for 4 hours.

Meanwhile, put the blueberries in a small pan with the water and cook until the berries begin to pop and turn glossy. Let cool, then let chill.

To serve, top each mousse with a few blueberries and a little white chocolate.

Makes 6

Mini Fruit Desserts

Make up the gelatine according to the package directions.

Divide the fruit between 6 plastic cups or glasses. Pour over the gelatine and let chill for 6 hours until firmly set.

Mix the yogurt with the vanilla extract and honey and spoon over the jellies.

Sprinkle with the nuts and serve.

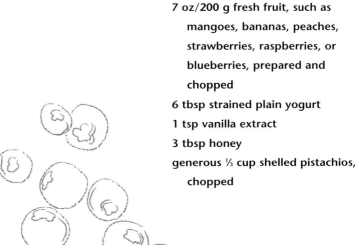

one ½-oz/12-g sachet
   sugar-free gelatine
7 oz/200 g fresh fruit, such as
   mangoes, bananas, peaches,
   strawberries, raspberries, or
   blueberries, prepared and
   chopped
6 tbsp strained plain yogurt
1 tsp vanilla extract
3 tbsp honey
generous ⅓ cup shelled pistachios,
   chopped

Makes 1 loaf

Banana Loaf

Preheat the oven to 350°F/180°C. Lightly grease and line a 1-lb/450-g loaf pan.

Sift the flours, sugar, a pinch of salt, and the spices into a large bowl.

In a separate bowl, mash the bananas with the orange juice, then stir in the eggs and oil. Pour into the dry ingredients and mix well.

Spoon into the prepared loaf pan and bake in the preheated oven for 1 hour, then test to see if it is cooked by inserting a skewer into the center. If it comes out clean, the loaf is done. If not, bake for an additional 10 minutes and test again.

Remove from the oven and let cool in the pan. Turn the loaf out, slice, and serve with honey, and sliced banana or chopped walnuts.

unsalted butter, for greasing
scant 1 cup white self-rising flour
scant ¾ cup light brown
    self-rising flour
generous ¾ cup packed raw
    brown sugar
½ tsp ground cinnamon
½ tsp ground nutmeg
2 large ripe bananas, peeled
¾ cup orange juice
2 eggs, beaten
4 tbsp canola oil
sea salt

To serve
honey
sliced banana or chopped walnuts

Baked Banana

Preheat the oven to 375°F/190°C. Make 2 slits along the length of the banana, cutting slightly into the flesh, and pull back the skin, but keep it attached at one end.

Push the chocolate buttons or chocolate flake into the slit and cover with the skin.

Wrap in foil. Keeping it upright, bake it in the preheated oven for 5–10 minutes until the chocolate has melted.

Remove from the foil and serve with yogurt.

1 banana, unpeeled
8 chocolate buttons or half
   a chocolate flake
plain yogurt, to serve

Makes 6

Fruity Phyllo Packages

Put the apples, golden raisins, nutmeg, and maple syrup in a small pan over a low heat and cook until the apples are soft. Leave to cool.

Preheat the oven to 375°F/190°C. Cut each sheet of phyllo pastry in half. Brush one half sparingly with a little oil, place another half on top, and brush the edges with a little oil. Spoon some of the apple mixture into the middle, pull in the edges, and scrunch to close, to form a little pastry bag. Place on a baking sheet. Repeat with the remaining phyllo pastry sheets and apple mixture to make 6 packages.

Brush the tops with a little more oil and bake in the preheated oven for 20 minutes until golden.

Remove from the oven and let cool slightly, then serve with yogurt.

3 apples, peeled, cored,
   and chopped
2 tbsp golden raisins
½ tsp ground nutmeg
1 tbsp maple syrup or honey
6 sheets phyllo pastry, thawed
   if frozen
peanut oil, for brushing
plain yogurt, to serve

Sticky Fruit Oaties

¾ cup/12 tbsp unsalted butter,
  plus extra for greasing
3 tbsp honey
generous ¾ cup packed raw
  brown sugar
3½ oz/100 g no-added-sugar
  smooth peanut butter
2¾ cups oatmeal
generous ¼ cup no-soak dried
  apricots, chopped
2 tbsp sunflower seeds
2 tbsp sesame seeds

Preheat the oven to 350°F/180°C. Grease and line an 8½-inch/22-cm square baking pan.

Melt the butter, honey, and sugar in a pan over low heat. When the sugar has melted, add the peanut butter, and stir until all the ingredients are well combined. Add all the remaining ingredients and mix well.

Press the mixture into the prepared pan and bake in the preheated oven for 20 minutes.

Remove from the oven and let cool in the pan, then cut into 16 squares.

Makes 6

Tropical Fruit Tarts

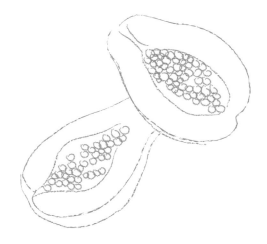

Preheat the oven to 350°F/180°C. Lightly oil 6 holes of a muffin pan.

Cut each sheet of phyllo pastry into quarters and brush each piece with a little oil. Layer 4 pieces one on top of the other, each at a slightly different angle, then press into a prepared muffin hole to make a rough-edged tart shell. Repeat with the remaining pieces of phyllo pastry to make 6 tart shells.

Bake in the preheated oven for 10 minutes until golden. Remove from the oven and let cool in the pan, then carefully transfer to a serving plate.

Fill each tart shell with the tropical fruit and litchis. Cut each passion fruit in half and scoop out the contents of each half onto a tart. Top with a few coconut curls.

peanut oil, for oiling
   and brushing
6 sheets phyllo pastry, thawed
   if frozen
mixed tropical fruit, such as papaya,
   mango, pineapple, banana, Cape
   gooseberry, prepared and diced
6 litchis, cut into ½-inch/1-cm dice
3 passion fruit
fresh coconut curls

Index

Apples
  Apple and Carrot Muffins 52
  Apple and Hazelnut Bread 31
  Apple Cake 99
  Buttered Cinnamon Apples on
    Fruit Toast 34
  Chicken and Apple Bites 48
Apricot and Sunflower Seed Cookies
  58
Avocado Dip 71

Bananas
  Baked Banana 122
  Banana Cinnamon Bread and
    Butter Pudding 105
  Banana Loaf 121
  Banana, Peach, and Strawberry
    Smoothie 25
  Mini Crunchy Banana Sandwiches
    67
  Orange and Banana Biscuits 59
Beans
  Burritos 88
  Sausage and Bean Casserole 91
  Spicy Bean Burgers 108
Berries, Very Berry Dessert 70
Bircher Granola 29
Blueberry Bran Muffins 20
Burritos 88
Butternut Squash, Couscous Salad
  with 60

Carrots
  Apple and Carrot Muffins 52
  Crispy Vegetable Bake 102
  Party Carrot Cake 73
Cheese
  Cheese and Herb Muffins 32
  Cheese Star Cookies 82
  Cherry Tomato and Cheese Tartlets
    57
  Sweet Potato, Cheese, and Leek
    Pie 90
Cherry Rascals 113
Chicken
  Chicken and Apple Bites 48
  Chicken and Leek Pie 97
  Chicken Nuggets 109
  Roasted Chicken and Sweet
    Potatoes 96

Sticky Drumsticks with Cucumber
  Salad 68
Chocolate Mousse Pots 118
Coconut Granola Squares 76
Couscous Salad with Roasted
  Butternut Squash 60
Cranberry and Pecan Slices 115
Crêpes, Almond and Golden Raisin
  22
Crumble
  Winter Fruit and Nut 104
Cupcakes, Cereal Fruit 26

Eggs
  Baked Eggs with Ham and Tomato
    35
  Spanish Omelet 51
  Sunshine Toast 23
  Tortillas with Tuna, Egg, and Corn
    46
English Muffin Pizzas 49

Jelly, Very Berry Jelly 70

Lollipops, Yogurt Lollipops 114

Mango and Papaya Smoothie
  25
Mashed Potato and Hamburger
  Casserole 93
Mini Fruit Desserts 119
Muffins
  Apple and Carrot 52
  Blueberry Bran 20
  Mini Cheese and Herb 32

Oaties, Sticky Fruit 124
Orange and Banana Biscuits 59

Party Straws 83
Pasta
  Creamy Pasta Bake 63
  Pasta Salad 54
  Roast Vegetable Lasagna 94
Phyllo Packages, Fruity 123
Pizza
  Easy Biscuit Pizzas 86
  English Muffin Pizzas 49
Plum Crisp 101
Porridge, Fruity Maple 37

Potatoes
  Crispy Vegetable Bake 102
  Souffléd Baked 45
  Spicy Potato Skins 71

Quiche, Mini Quiches 74

Raspberries
  Almond and Golden Raisin Crêpes
    with 22
  Raspberry Fool 100

Salmon Fishcakes 89
Sandwiches and Wraps 53
  Burritos 88
  Mini Crunchy Banana 67
  Pinwheel 80
  Pita Pockets with Hummus and
    Salad 44
  Tortillas with Tuna, Egg, and
    Corn 46
Sausages
  Honey Sesame 66
  Sausage and Bean Casserole 91
Skewers, Fruit Skewers 110
Smoothies 25
Stir-Fry, Sesame Noodle 43
Strawberries
  Banana, Peach, and Strawberry
    Smoothie 25
  Mini Cheesecakes 116
  Strawberry Cupcakes 79
Sweet Potatoes
  Roasted Chicken and 96
  Sweet Potato, Cheese, and Leek Pie
    90

Tarts, Tropical Fruit 127
Tomatoes
  Baked Eggs with Ham and 35
  Cherry Tomato and Cheese Tartlets
    57
  Creamy Tomato Soup 40
Tuna
  Bites 77
  Tortillas with Tuna, Egg, and Corn 46

Yogurt
  Crunchy 28
  Lollies 114